The
Belfast
Mural
Guide

ISBN: 978-0-9568069-3-2

The contents of this publication are believed correct at the time of printing. Nevertheless, the publishers cannot be held responsible for any errors or omissions or for changes in the details given in this guide, or for the consequences for any reliance on the information provided by the same. Assessments regarding the inclusion, or exclusion, of sites of interest and so forth are based on the authors own experience and therefore descriptions and opinions given in this guide contain an element of subjective opinion which may not necessarily reflect the publishers' opinion or dictate a readers own experience on another occasion. We have tried to ensure accuracy in this guide, but things do change and we would be grateful if readers would advise us of any inaccuracies they may encounter.

Published by MSF Press
Maps, Text and Photographs © MSF Press
MSF Press retains the copyright in the original edition © 2014 and in all subsequent editions, reprints and amendments.
2nd Edition
email: msfpress@googlemail.com
Layout & Design by MSF Press
Printed by Nova Print
155 Northumberland Street
Belfast BT13 2JF

The walls of Belfast have been often described as an open air art gallery. Indeed there are many interesting and beautifully painted murals throughout the city, all of which have a story to tell. The object of this short book is to provide a guide to some of the many murals which make up the sites of political, historical and cultural interest across Belfast. Taking Belfast City Hall as a starting point, we have focused on those murals which are within a realistic walking distance or can be easily reached through public transport. The locations of these murals will, in many instances, reveal other murals, sculptures and plaques which may be of interest to visitors. For the purpose of this book repetitively themed or badly deteriorated murals have been largely excluded. It should also be noted that murals are subject to change. Factors such as developing political issues, both local and international, and the effect of weather on older murals, all play their part. However, although the theme of a mural may change, it is often replaced by a new and thought provoking image at the same location. All that remains to say is:

Welcome to Belfast
Enjoy the City
Enjoy the Art

Fáilte go Béal Feirste
Bain sult as an Chathair
Bain sult as an Ealaín

Finn McCool

Adorning the front facade of the West Belfast Taxi Association's Passenger Terminal is Belfast's tallest mural. Standing more than ten meters tall, is the famed giant, Finn McCool (Fionn mac Cumhaill) and his wife Sadhbh. There are many accounts of his life in Celtic Mythology the most well known story is his fight with the

Scottish Giant at the Causeway but the scene depicted here tells of how Sadhbh, a beautiful young woman, was transformed into a fawn by a druid. Fionn unaware of this, captured the deer while hunting. On reaching the safety of his fort, Sadhbh returned to her human form and for as long as she remained there, the spell remained broken. They married, and Sadhbh became pregnant,

4

before the child was born, the druid using trickery, lured her from her home, and she once more became a fawn. Fionn spent many years searching for his wife but she was never seen again. He did however discover a young boy, Oisín, who had been raised by a deer and who he recognised as his son. It is said that Oisín became a warrior and Ireland's greatest poet. There are varying accounts of Fionn's death  and one that states that Fionn never died, rather he sleeps in a cave deep below the earth and will one day return to defend Ireland in her hour of greatest need.

The West Belfast Taxi Association on whose building the mural is painted, is a community based project, which, for more than 40 years, has provided a 'Taxi Bus' service and through their tour sub group, 'Taxitrax', they are the originator of the famous Black Taxi Tour.

Tours can be booked through their Passenger Terminal at King Street or Tel: 028 90315777; Out of office hours Mobile: 07892716660

Location: King Street
Distance from City Hall: 500m/.3 miles.
Walking Time: 5 mins
GPS: N 54° 35. 997′   W 5° 56. 079′

Duke of York

Outside the Duke of York pub in Commercial Court, is a small courtyard which is home to some of Belfast's popular street art. Located just off Donegall Street, in this pedestrianised passageway, are some 2 and 3 dimensional murals by Belfast artist Ciaran Gallagher, which captures many of Belfast's citizens, celebrities and landmarks, as well as some well-known international visitors. World famous guitarist Rory Gallagher can be found alongside singer, Van Morrison, and footballer George Best along with a host of other Irish celebrities. A tongue-in-cheek mural pokes fun at Unionist flag protesters outside Belfast's City Hall, while, against a backdrop of the Harland & Wolff cranes, Albert Clock and the much bombed €uropa Hotel, Bill Clinton can be seen at the

hotel's window. A bikini clad Rhianna, looks out from yet another. As you take in the 3D artwork, painted in the style of Austrian film maker Fritz Lang, try to place names to the faces of those featured in the mural but don't forget to check out the ceiling, it too has artwork in the form of the W. B. Yeats poem 'An Irish Airman Foresees His Death.'

Location: Commercial Court
Distance from City Hall: 1.3 km/0.8 miles.
Walking Time: 16 mins
GPS: N 54° 36. 099´   W 5° 55. 633´

Bank Square

North Street

Lower North Street

Library Street

Donegall Street

'Culture Night'

Late September sees approximately over 50,000 people converge on Belfast's city centre to celebrate 'Culture night' when more than 200 culture based events are staged in over 100 locations. Music and Theatre are around every corner, so too is the Art. Over 30 murals created for the event can be seen on the walls and shop fronts of Belfast.

Location: Donegall St & City Centre
Distance from City Hall: 900m/0.5 miles.
Walking Time: 9 mins
GPS: N 54° 36. 242′ W 5° 55. 852′

John Peel
1939-2004

Teenage Dreams

Located in the Cathedral Quarter of Belfast is a small mural of BBC disc jockey and radio presenter John Peel. Elsewhere in the city, beneath an East Belfast flyover at Bridge End, are his favourite lyrics , "Teenage dreams, so hard to beat", from "Teenage Kicks" by Derry band, The Undertones. After Peels death in 2004 the lyrics were painted on the flyover in east Belfast, however, when the local council painted over them as part of a regeneration programme, there was public outcry. Two years later, the mural was reinstated by the Council and painted by the original artist with the assistance of local youth clubs.

Location: Commercial Court
Distance from City Hall: 1.3 km/0.8 miles.
Walking Time: 16 mins
GPS: N 54° 36. 099′   W 5° 55. 633′

Welcome to West Belfast

Located within yards of Divis Tower, is this colourful mural which draws on aspects of Celtic mythology and merges it with images of all that is positive in the community: the youth of West Belfast, the music and Irish Dancing as well as significant buildings such as the Irish language centre, Culturlann and Clonard Monastery. It is worth noting that in 1972 the British Army occupied the top two floors of Divis Tower. Observation posts were placed on the roof and people's homes were turned into a heavily fortified base. For more than three decades this military installation

Location: Divis Street
Distance from City Hall: 1 km/0.6 miles.
Walking Time: 13 mins
GPS: N 54° 35. 012´ W 5° 56. 531´

physically dominated the area. It was not until March 2005 that British soldiers finally withdrew from the flats. Directly opposite this mural is part of

> I ndil cbaimbne
> This plaque is dedicated
> to the memory of
> PATRICK ROONEY aged 9
> HUGH McCABE aged 20
> who were murdered in this vicinity
> by the R.U.C. on 15th August 1969
>
> A mhuire Banrion
> Na Ngael Guigh ortbu

the 'Peace Wall' which divides the city. Located on the side of Divis Tower is a small plaque dedicated to two local people who were shot dead by the Royal Ulster Constabulary in August 1969: nine year old Patrick Rooney who was killed as he lay in bed and Hugh McCabe, a local man, and serving British soldier who was also shot dead by the Royal Ulster Constabulary as he went to the aid of a wounded man.

The International Wall

The wall, of what was once an old flour mill, situated at the corner of Divis and Northumberland Street, has become one of Belfast's most recognisable features - the International Wall. This stretch of wall consisting of more than 30 murals reflects the views and sympathies of the people of West Belfast. The Street Art at this location is very political and the themes reflect current local and international issues.

Location: Divis Street/Northumberland Street
Distance from City Hall: 1.3 km/0.8 miles.
Walking Time: 16 mins
GPS: N 54° 35. 975´ W 5° 56. 791´

Easter Rising 1916-2016

On Easter Monday 1916, armed detachments of the Irish Volunteers, the Irish Citizen Army, Cumann na mban and na Fianna h-Éireann seized strategic positions around Dublin. Outside the General Post Office, Patrick Pearse, as President of the Provisional Government, read out a Proclamation and in doing so declared Ireland a sovereign independent nation. To mark the centenary of that event, the murals of the International Wall were repainted to provide an insight into the circumstances which lead to the Rising. The section of the wall shown above focuses on the role of women.

Location: International Wall, Divis Street
Distance from City Hall: 1.3 km/0.8 miles.
Walking Time: 16 mins
GPS: N 54° 35. 983´ W 5° 56. 750´

The 1981 Hunger Strike

In late 1980, protests in the prisons had reached their height. For five years republican prisoners had protested against the denial of political status for imprisoned combatants in the H Blocks of Long Kesh and in Armagh women's prison. Conditions in both prisons had deteriorated and the protest escalated to the point whereby the prisoners embarked on a Hunger Strike in 1980. As one of the prisoners, Sean McKenna, lapsed into unconsciousness, the British Government, through intermediaries offered a solution; end the Hunger strike and a new enlightened prison regime would be created; the new regime, they said, would contain enough reforms to satisfy the prisoners. The Hunger Strike ended but the reforms were not implemented. The prisoners were faced with a dilemma; accept defeat and with it criminalisation, or resist. On the 1st March 1981, Bobby

---

Location: International Wall, Divis Street
Distance from City Hall: 1.3 km/.8 miles.
Walking Time: 16 mins
GPS: N 54° 35. 989´ W 5° 56. 728´

Sands, the Officer Commanding the IRA prisoners embarked on a Hunger Strike, and was followed in stages by others. One by one ten men died in the prison. The coloured portraits in this mural show the faces of those who died in the H Blocks that year: Bobby Sands, Francis Hughes, Raymond McCreesh, Patsy O'Hara, Joe McDonnell, Martin Hurson, Kevin Lynch, Kieran Doherty, Tom McElwee and Micky Devine. The black and white images show Michael Gaughan and Frank Stagg who died on Hunger Strike in 1974 and 1976 in Parkhurst and Wakefield Prisons in England. The mural was painted to marked the 30th anniversary of the '81 Hunger Strike.

1916 - 1972

The image of the five young men, all dressed in the attire of 1916, gives little indication as to who they were or why they are featured at the International Wall. This mural, repainted with a 1916 theme is dedicated to the memory of five members of the IRA who were part of the local community and who died in September and October 1972. The men portrayed in the mural are Jimmy Quigley and Danny McAreavey who were both shot dead by British soldiers and Joe McKinney, Paddy Pendelton and John Donaghy who all died when a bomb they were assembling, exploded prematurely. In the background of the mural can be seen the twin spires of St Peters Cathedral which is located opposite the mural.

Location: Divis Street
Distance from City Hall: 1.3 km/.8 miles
Walking Time: 16 mins
GPS: N 54° 35. 987′ W 5° 56. 736′

Francis Hughes

Francis Hughes, from the South Derry town of Bellaghy, is central to this mural which marked the 30th anniversary of the 1981 Hunger Strike. Seriously wounded and captured during a gun battle with British soldiers, Francis was to follow Bobby Sands as the second IRA member to go on Hunger Strike. He died fifty nine days later on the 12th May, aged 25. The mural places him in the context of history and surrounds him with his fellow Hunger Strikers and with Republicans from previous eras such as James Connolly, Pádraig Pearse and Roger Casement who were executed in 1916 and the father of Irish Republicanism, Theobald Wolfe Tone who died in prison in 1798.

Location: International Wall,Northumberland Street
Distance from City Hall: 1.3 km/.8 miles.
Walking Time: 16 mins
GPS: N 54° 35. 991´ W 5° 56. 802´

Climate Change

Commissioned by the Irish Charity 'Trócaire', this mural promotes the message that Climate Change unfairly affects poor and vulnerable communities around the world and is the cause of drought, hunger and poverty. Using the imagery of an hourglass, the mural is placed in a Belfast context, with the inclusion of such sights as the Albert Clock, Harland and Wolff Cranes and the Titanic Belfast Centre. Central to the mural is the painting "Der Schrei der Natur" ("The Scream of Nature") by Norwegian artist Edvard Munch, which has been incorporated into the mural in the form of a map of the world.

Location: International Wall, Divis Street
Distance from City Hall: 1.3 km/0.8 miles.
Walking Time: 16 mins
GPS: N 54° 36. 018´ W 5° 56. 825´

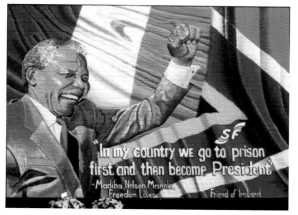

Nelson Mandela

Nelson Mandela, former political prisoner and president of South Africa, has a special place in the hearts of freedom loving people throughout the world. West Belfast shares this view of a man who fought for the Freedom of his own nation. In 2013, in the days before his 95th birthday, and as he lay gravely ill, Irish Republicans unveiled this mural, to a man who was both a friend to Ireland and who inspired the world. Mandela's portrait is set against the Irish and South African flags and in a reference to the influence of political prisoners, it carries his famous, and often smile raising quote, 'In my country we go to prison first and then become President'. Nelson Mandela died on the 5th December 2013.

Location: International Wall,Northumberland Street
Distance from City Hall: 1.3 km/.8 miles.
Walking Time: 16 mins
GPS: N 54° 35. 986´ W 5° 56. 799´

Frederick Douglass

Frederick Douglass was born into slavery in 1818 and was one of the foremost leaders of the abolitionist movement, which fought to end slavery within the United States in the decades prior to the American Civil War. Inspired by two Irishmen to escape from slavery, Douglass came to Ireland during the famine. Henceforth he championed the abolition of slavery, women's rights and Irish freedom. Renown for his eloquence, he toured and lectured on the brutality and immorality of slavery.

Location: International Wall,Northumberland Street
Distance from City Hall: 1.3 km/.8 miles.
Walking Time: 16 mins
GPS: N 54° 36. 037´ W 5° 56. 836´

Palestinian Solidarity

Murals which highlight the plight of the Palestinian people are a common sight in the Republican areas of Belfast and are a permanent feature of the International Wall. The murals, which are commissioned by a local solidarity group, are changed periodically to reflect events in Palestine. Past murals have focused on events such as the foundation of the Israeli state; Israeli air strikes on Gaza, Hunger Strikes and the plight of Palestinian prisoners.

The above mural located in Northumberland Street expresses the solidarity between Palestinian and Irish Republican prisoners

Location: International Wall,Northumberland Street
Distance from City Hall: 1.3 km/.8 miles.
Walking Time: 16 mins
GPS: N 54° 36. 018´ W 5° 56. 823´

Falls Memorial Garden

The Falls Memorial Garden, located approximately one hundred yards from the International Wall, on the main Falls Road, was one of the first memorial gardens of its kind in Belfast. It was opened in June 2001 and is dedicated to the memory of local IRA members and residents of the area who died during the conflict. The garden, which contains a water feature, provides a sheltered and relaxing place to sit and reflect. The mural overlooking the garden contains images of young IRA men from the area who died on Active Service. A map of the area, as it looked in the early 1970's, pinpoints the locations where they died.

Location: Falls Road
Distance from City Hall: 1.6 km/1 mile.
Walking Time: 20 mins
GPS: N 54° 35. 927′ W 5° 57. 009′

The Falls Library

The Falls library was gifted to the City of Belfast in 1908 by the Scottish American philanthropist Andrew Carnegie , who believed that libraries should be free and thereby available to all. However, the building did not always function as Carnegie had intended. In the early 1920's the library was taken over by the Royal Irish Constabulary (RIC) and used as a temporary barracks. In order to protect the library, which is a listed building, the mural, which was once displayed in the East Harlem area of New York to mark the 20th anniversary of the 1981 Hunger Strike, was digitally transferred on to canvas. Close examination of the mural reveals that it is not just a tribute to Irish Hunger Strikers, but to all those who struggled for justice throughout the world. The border contains images of Nelson Mandela, Martin Luther King, Leonard Peltier, Ghandi, as well as Irish Republicans, Nora Connolly, Mairéad Farrell, Michael Gaughan and Frank Stagg.

> Location: Falls Road
> Distance from City Hall: 1.6 km/1 mile.
> Walking Time: 20 mins
> GPS: N 54° 35. 891´ W 5° 57. 133´

Bobby Sands

Bobby Sands, died in the H-Blocks of Long Kesh on the 5th May 1981 after 66 days on Hunger Strike. As an IRA Volunteer and the Officer Commanding the republican prisoners, he was the first of ten men to die in the prison that year. In an effort to pressurise the British government and save the lives of those on Hunger Strike, it was decided that, as a prisoner, he should stand for election to Westminster. On the 9th April he was elected as a Member of Parliament, receiving over 30,000 votes, which was more votes than the British Prime Minister of the time, Margaret Thatcher, received in her own constituency. The Bobby Sands mural, painted by local artist Dan Devenny, is located at the corner of Sevastopol Street and the Falls Road and is without doubt the most photographed mural in Belfast.

Location: Sevastapol Street
Distance from City Hall: 1.7 km/1.1 miles.
Walking Time: 22 mins
GPS: N 54° 35. 872´ W 5° 57. 163´

The Ulster Tower

The Ulster Tower, located at Thiepval Wood, and site of the Battle of the Somme in France, was unveiled on the 19th November 1921. The monument was dedicated to the men of the 36th Ulster Division who died there and is a replica of Helen's Tower in the Clandeboye Estate in Bangor. Helen's Tower inspired the Somme monument because it was there that the newly formed 36th Division trained before their departure to France and it would have been a familiar sight to many of the 5,000 members of the Ulster Division who died at the Somme on the 1st July 1916. The Thiepval Monument was unveiled by Field Marshall Sir Henry Wilson, in 1921 and who himself was assassinated by the IRA at his London home in June 1922 following the partition of Ireland.

Location: Hopewell Avenue
Distance from City Hall: 1.9 km/1.2 miles.
Walking Time: 24 mins
GPS: N 54° 36. 452´ W 5° 56. 715´

Ulster Volunteer Force

The Ulster Volunteer Force was formed in 1966 to combat what it perceived to be a rise in support for Irish Republicanism and the organisation stated that known IRA men would be "executed mercilessly and without hesitation.' In total the organisation was responsible for killing more than 500 people during the troubles, the vast majority of whom were Catholics who had no connection with the IRA. This Shankill Road Mural is dedicated to five local men; Robert McIntyre, Robert Wadsworth, Thomas Chapman, James McGregor and William Hanna. All are described as being members of 'C' Company, 1st Battalion, Ulster Volunteer Force.

Location: Carnan Street/Shankill Road
Distance from City Hall: 2.2 km/1.4 miles.
Walking Time: 28 mins
GPS: N 54° 36. 261′ W 5° 57. 249′

Summer of '69

In 1966, the loyalist paramilitary organisation, the Ulster Volunteer Force, was formed. By June they had killed two Catholic men and a Protestant woman. Throughout the 1960's the demand for Civil Rights grew: electoral and voting malpractices as well as inequalities in housing allocation needed to be addressed. In an attempt to halt reforms, the UVF tried to create the illusion of an active IRA, by carrying out a series of bomb attacks in early 1969. The ruse failed. As more students and civil rights activists took to the streets and peaceful protest marches were met by with violence by state forces, conflict was only a short time away. August 1969 saw the 'Troubles' erupted on to the streets. In Belfast eight people died and another 750 were injured. This mural remembers that time. Conflict and attacks on homes saw the displacement of 1,505 Catholic and 315 Protestant families

Location: Hopewell Avenue
Distance from City Hall: 1.9 km/1.2 miles.
Walking Time: 24 mins
GPS: N 54° 36. 452′ W 5° 56. 715′

Stevie 'Topgun' McKeag

A portrait of Steven McKeag, is central to this Shankill Road mural. McKeag, who died in September 2000 is described on the mural as being the Military Commander of the UFF (Ulster Freedom Fighters) in the Shankill area. His nickname 'Topgun' is said to come from an annual award ceremony held by the loyalist paramilitary group in which the person who carried out the most killings during the previous year was awarded the title. It is claimed that McKeag was awarded the title every year. A number of published sources have quoted anonymous sources within the UDA/UFF of saying that he was responsible for the deaths of at least 12 Catholic men and women.

Location: Hopewell Crescent
Distance from City Hall: 1.9 km/1.2 miles.
Walking Time: 24 mins
GPS: N 54° 36. 365´ W 5° 56. 534´

Gold Rush

This community based mural, makes reference to an event in 1969, which occurred during the demolition of old Victorian tenement buildings at Christopher Street,   As the redevelopment of the area took place and the wreckers ball smashed into the old homes, an unknown number of gold sovereigns spilled out into the street. Word quickly spread throughout the area that a treasure trove had been discovered and hundreds of local children, black from the dust, scrambled through the ruins, in their hunt for gold. It is not known the value of the coins discovered that day but it is believed that most of those unearthed were taken home by the children, who no doubt were both praised and scolded for their efforts.

Location: Hopewell Crescent
Distance from City Hall: 1.9 km/1.2 miles.
Walking Time: 24 mins
GPS: N 54° 36. 358´ W 5° 56. 396´

William McCullough

Ulster Defence Association member William 'Bucky' McCullough is the subject of this Shankill Road mural. McCullough, is said to have joined the UDA at its inception . The mural states that McCullough held the rank of Lieutenant-Colonel within his organisation and the columns to the right and left of his image list the names of twenty deceased members of the UDA. McCullough was shot dead by members of the Irish National Liberation Army (INLA) in 1981. In 1999, McCullough's son, Alan, was shot dead as the direct result of a feud which was taking place within the UDA.

Location: Hopewell Crescent
Distance from City Hall: 1.9 km/1.2 miles.
Walking Time: 24 mins
GPS: N 54° 36. 358´ W 5° 56. 396´

Jackie Coulter

August 2000 saw tensions between the Ulster Defence Association and the Ulster Volunteer Force come to a head in the form of a feud between the two Loyalist groups. Intimidation was widespread. Over the next four months seven people were killed and more than 200 families were displaced. The first of these to be killed was Jackie Coulter, who was shot dead alongside a friend on the 21st August 2000 on Belfast's Crumlin Road. The mural states that Coulter was a member of C Company of the UDA and that he was murdered by the UVF.

Location: Shankill Parade
Distance from City Hall: 1.9 km/1.2 miles.
Walking Time: 24 mins
GPS: N 54° 36. 311´ W 5° 56. 473´

'NEVER DOUBT that a small group of thoughtful, concerned citizens can CHANGE THE WORLD.

Indeed it is the only thing that ever has.'

Margaret Mead,
American Author 1901–1978

Never Doubt

Significant changes have been made to many Shankill Road murals due to redevelopment of the area. Reimaging of the Community has been an on-going project, with many of the existing loyalist murals being replaced by murals which promote social change and the hopes of youth and women. The above digitally produced mural takes a local map and overlays it with a quote from American cultural anthropologist Margaret Mead "Never doubt that a small group of thoughtful concerned citizens can change the world. Indeed it is the only thing that ever has.' The mural's history, along with photos of the old, murals are provided on notice boards.

Location: Hopewell Avenue
Distance from City Hall: 1.9 km/1.2 miles.
Walking Time: 24 mins
GPS: N 54° 36. 437′ W 5° 56. 391s′

SINCE 1970 SEVENTEEN PEOPLE KILLED-INCLUDING 8 CHILDREN

Plastic Bullets

Plastic bullets, and their predecessor, rubber bullets, have since their introduction in 1971, claimed the lives of seventeen people from across the North. Hundreds more have received serious injuries; some have been blinded for life. This mural, located at the junction of Islandbawn Street and the Falls Road, puts faces to the names of those killed and is a public demand that these weapons be removed from our streets. The youngest victim of a plastic and rubber bullet was only 10 years of age. To help visualise these 'innocent' sounding bullets, the above

photograph shows both bullets in the hands of a 10 year old boy.

Location: Islandbawn Street
Distance from City Hall: 2.6 km/1.6 miles.
Walking Time: 33 mins
GPS: N 54° 35. 529′ W 5° 57. 733′

Easter Rising 1916

The Easter Rising of 1916 was a major turning point in Irish history. This mural shows a member of the Irish Volunteers outside the General Post Office in Dublin during the Rising. Also in the mural are the emblems of the four provinces of Ireland, Ulster, Munster, Leinster and Connacht. The Easter lily in the mural signifies the sacrifice of the men and women who have died fighting for the establishment of an Irish Republic.

Central to the 1916 mural at Beechmount Avenue is a plaque on which is inscribed a Roll of Honour and lists the names of seven republican activists who died between 1972 and 1996

Location: Beechmount Avenue
Distance from City Hall: 2.8 km/1.8 miles.
Walking Time: 35 mins
GPS: N 54° 35. 513´ W 5° 57. 528´

HUMAN RIGHTS ACTIVIST
Pat Finucane
1949-1989
TARGETED BY BRITISH ESTABLISHMENT
EXECUTED BY UNIONIST DEATH SQUADS

"......If you don't defend
human rights lawyers
who will defend
human rights?-*ROSEMARY NELSON*

Pat Finucane

Human Rights lawyer Pat Finucane was shot dead at his
North Belfast home by members of the Ulster Defence
Association on 12th February 1989. The shooting came less
than four weeks after British MP, Douglas Hogg, then
Parliamentary Under-Secretary of State, claimed "that there
are in Northern Ireland a number of solicitors who are unduly
sympathetic to the cause of the IRA." In subsequent
investigations into this killing it emerged that that the British
Security Forces had several agents operating within the
UDA. Some of these agents were directly involved in killing
Pat Finucane and it is widely believed he was a victim of
State sponsored murder. The mural carries a quote from
human rights lawyer Rosemary Nelson, who herself was
assassinated by loyalists in 1999, "...if you don't defend
human rights lawyers who will defend human rights?".

Location: Beechmount Drive
Distance from City Hall: 2.8 km/1.8 miles.
Walking Time: 35 mins
GPS: N 54° 35. 501´ W 5° 57. 854´

Collusion Wall

The Collusion Wall at Beechmount Avenue, whilst not a mural as such but a public exhibition relating to the issue of British state forces colluding with loyalist paramilitary organisations, it is worth visiting in order to gain an understanding of the human cost of war.

Throughout the conflict claims were often made by Republicans that the RUC and British Army carried out political assassinations or directed loyalist death squads to act on their behalf. As a matter of course these claims were dismissed as republican propaganda, however the belief has continued to gain strength.

Location: Beechmount Avenue
Distance from City Hall: 3 km/1.9 miles.
Walking Time: 38 mins
GPS: N 54° 35. 685´ W 5° 57. 711´

James Connolly

The above mural, dedicated to James Connolly and his daughter Nora Connolly O'Brien, is located only yards from what was their family home. Widely recognised as being one of the greatest political thinkers to emerge in twentieth century Ireland, Connolly came to Belfast as a union organiser in 1911. When the secret military council of the Irish Republican Brotherhood decided to embark on an armed rising in 1916, Connolly, who was then living in Dublin, was taken into their confidence. Badly wounded during the fighting at Dublin's GPO he was, as a member of the Provisional Government, brought before a British military tribunal and was sentenced to death. On the 12th May 1916, unable to stand he was carried to the stone breakers' yard in Kilmainham Gaol. It was there he was strapped to a chair and executed by firing squad.

Location: Clondara Street
Distance from City Hall: 3.4 km/2.1 miles.
Walking Time: 43 mins
GPS: N 54° 35. 305′ W 5° 58. 205′

Kieran Doherty

Andersonstown was home to IRA Volunteer and Hunger Striker Kieran Doherty. This mural located a short distance from his home, is one of many which pay tribute to him. 'Big Doc' as he was known to his friends and comrades was a keen sportsman and played Gaelic football for St Teresa's Gaelic Athletic Club. Arrested in 1976 and sentenced to 18 years in prison, Kieran joined the 'Blanket Protest' and later the Hunger Strike. On the 11th June 1981 a General Election was called and Kieran, along with other Republican prisoners, stood as Anti H-Block candidates. He was elected by the people of Cavan–Monaghan to represent them in Leinster House. Kieran died on the 2nd August 1981 after 72 days on Hunger Strike. He was aged 27.

Location: Slemish Way/Andersonstown Road
Distance from City Hall: 5.5 km/3.4 miles
Walking Time: 67 mins
GPS: N 54° 34. 458´ W 5° 59. 160´

The Great Hunger

This mural, painted in black and white, rejects the claim of a natural famine occurring from 1845-47 with the simple message: 'Nature sent the potato blight. Government and landlords created the famine.' Ireland of 1845, was a country with a population of approximately 8 million people, however by 1850 this had dropped by 25%. One million people had died of starvation and a further one million emigrating to Britain, the United States, Canada and Australia. Starvation, had set in motion a culture of emigration which would continue well into the next century.

Location: Lenadoon Avenue
Distance from City Hall: 7.1 km/4.4miles.
Walking Time: 92 mins
GPS: N 54° 34. 286′ W 6° 00. 613′

Julie Livingstone

On the 12th May 1981, in the hours after the death of Francis Hughes on hunger strike, street protests broke out in nationalist areas. One such protest took place in the Lenadoon area of Belfast. Fourteen year old Julie Livingstone, whose portrait adorns this Lenadoon wall and a young friend, were returning home from an errand to a local shop. The children had just passed through the peaceful protest when two military vehicles arrived on the scene and as they passed the protestors, two plastic bullets were fired. Julie was struck on the head and was rushed to hospital. She died the following day. An inquest into her death concluded that she was an innocent victim. The soldier who fired the fatal shot was never charged with any offence.

Location: Glenveagh Drive
Distance from City Hall: 7.1 km/4.4miles.
Walking Time: 92 mins
GPS: N 54° 34. 521′ W 6° 01. 278′

Dublin, Easter 1916

'Freedom Fighters outside the GPO' is the name given to this Whiterock Road mural. Clearly identifiable in the mural are James Connolly and Pádraig Pearse who were both executed for their part in the Rising. To the centre is the figure of Constance Gore Booth, who is more commonly known as Countess Markievicz. Between 1919 and 1921 she held the position of Minister of Labour in the First Dáil (parliament) and was the first woman cabinet minister. Constance died in 1927 at the age of 57. It is said that the poor of Dublin lined the streets for her funeral. She is buried in Glasnevin Cemetery in Dublin.

Location:Whiterock Road
Distance from City Hall: 4.8 km/3miles.
Walking Time: 64 mins
GPS: N 54° 35. 589′ W 5° 59. 097′

Dedicated to Vols
- Bobby McCrudden,
Mundo O'Rawe
Pearse Jordan -

*In passing this mural, pause a little while,
Pray for us and Erin, Then Smile*

Ballymurphy

Throughout the Ballymurphy area of Belfast and in particular on Ballymurphy Road, Ballymurphy Crescent, Glenalina Road and Divismore Crescent, there are a series of murals dedicated to members of the Irish Republican Army who were killed during the conflict. The above mural, located next to the Ballymurphy Memorial Garden, is one such mural and remembers three local men Bobby McCrudden, Mundo O'Rawe and Pearse Jordan.

Location: Divismore Crescent
Distance from City Hall: 4.8 km/3 miles.
Walking Time: 60 mins
GPS: N 54° 35. 735′   W 5° 59. 082′

Cumann na mBan

Cumann na mBan, (Irishwomen's Council) was established in Dublin in 1914 and mirrored the structures of the Irish Volunteers. Easter week 1916 saw its members participate in the Rising. In 1922 its membership opposed the treaty with Britain and in the civil war which followed, sided with the anti-treaty forces. When the Republican Movement split in 1916 the organisation aligned itself with the Provisional IRA and between 1971 and 1976 ten of its members lost their lives in the conflict. This colourful mural has as its theme the women of Cumann na mBan and is dedicated to six local republican women; Maura Meehan and her sister Dorothy Maguire, Anne Marie Pettigrew, Anne Parker, Catherine McGartland and 14 year old Eileen Mackin.

Location: Ballymurphy Road
Distance from City Hall: 4.2 km/2.6 miles.
Walking Time: 55 mins
GPS: N 54° 35. 545′ W 5° 58. 840′

Óglaigh na hÉireann

Located at Glenalina Road in West Belfast, this mural is dedicated to members of the IRA from Ballymurphy who lost their lives in the conflict. The mural is surrounded by ornate railing on which are inscribed the words Óglaigh na h-Éireann. The name Óglaigh na h-Éireann, which is translated as Volunteers of Ireland, is the Gaelic name which, although not a literal translation, has been used by the IRA since its formation. The mural shows a number of armed IRA members patrolling the streets of Ballymurphy while local republicans who provided them with support can be seen looking on.

Location: Glenalina Road
Distance from City Hall: 4.8 km/3 mile
Walking Time: 60 mins
GPS: N 54° 35. 616´ W 5° 59. 014´

Jim Bryson

Jim Bryson and Patrick Mulvenna were members of the IRA's Belfast Brigade. On 31st August 1973, British soldiers, concealed in a secret observation post mounted an ambushed as the men drove through the Ballymurphy area of Belfast. Patrick Mulvenna was killed instantly. Jim Bryson, who escaped the previous year from the Maidstone prison ship where he had been interned and from Crumlin Road Jail, died three weeks later on the 22nd September. In the mural Bryson is pictured carrying a Lewis machine gun.

Location: Ballymurphy Road
Distance from City Hall: 4.5 km/2.8 miles.
Walking Time: 59 mins
GPS: N 54° 35. 685´ W 5° 58. 829´

Ballymurphy Massacre

In August 1971, in the days that followed the introduction of internment, British Paratroopers shot dead eleven people in the Ballymurphy area. Among those they shot dead was a Catholic priest as he gave the 'Last Rights' to a dying man. The mural, depicts this scene and includes portraits of all eleven victims. Located directly below the main mural are a number of smaller ones in which the families of those who were shot dead, under the banner 'Time for Truth Time for Justice' demand an independent international investigation into all the deaths and for the British Government to issue a statement of innocence and a public apology. The murals clearly shows the impact on the families by stating that 57 children lost a parent in the massacre.

Location: Springfield Road
Distance from City Hall: 5 km/3.1 miles.
Walking Time: 66 mins
GPS: N 54° 35. 693´ W 5° 59. 210´

Nuada of the Silver Arm

This elaborate and colourful mural by takes its inspiration from the artwork of Jim Fitzpatrick. Central to the mural, which tells of the mythical 'Tuatha Dé Danann' (people of the goddess Danu), is Nuada, their first king. It is said that Nuada had been their king for seven years before they came to Ireland. Legend has it that he lost his arm in battle but the loss of a limb rendered him less than perfect and as such he was no longer eligible to be king. A physician is said to have made Nuada a functioning arm out of silver and later one made of flesh and blood. Restored, he once more became king and ruled for a further 20 years. Nuada was finally killed and beheaded in battle by the Fomorian giant, 'Balor of the Evil Eye'. His death was avenged by his appointed successor Lugh.

Location: Whiterock Road
Distance from City Hall: 4.8 km/3miles.
Walking Time: 64 mins
GPS: N 54° 35. 673´ W 5° 59. 256´

Mass Graves of Ireland

This mural is dedicated to the men, women and children who died of starvation during the Great Hunger and it states that it is wrong to call this period in Irish history 'a famine' for it 'dishonours the pain and untold suffering our ancestors endured'. The mural also points out that between 1845 and 1852 the British Government seized at gunpoint and took the food of the land for profit while the people starved. Livestock, flour, grain, meat, poultry and dairy products were exported on British warships. The mural states that between 40 and 70 shiploads of food left Ireland each day under armed escort. Enough food to sustain 18 million people.

Location: Springfield Road
Distance from City Hall: 5.6 km/3.5 miles.
Walking Time: 73 mins
GPS: N 54° 35. 834´ W 5° 58. 746´

Springhill Massacre

On the 9th July 1972, British Army snipers, positioned in a timber yard overlooking the Springhill housing estate, shot dead five local people. Justifying the shootings they claimed that all those killed were members of the IRA. It was a claim which was rejected by the victims' families. The British Army's versions of events is clearly at odds with what local people experienced. However, some facts are beyond dispute; between 8.30pm and 1.00am, five people including two children and a priest were shot dead. For more than 40 years the victims families, supported by the community, sought justice and continue to campaigned for an independent investigation into the massacre.

Location: Springfield Road :
Distance from City Hall: 5.6 km/3.5 miles.
Walking Time: 73 mins
GPS: N 54° 35. 834´ W 5° 58. 746´

Brian Stewart

On the 4th October 1976 thirteen year old Brian Stewart was shot by a British soldier close to his home. Eye witnesses have stated that they saw a number of children playing in the street when a British soldier, a member of the Kings Own Scottish Borders who was on foot patrol in the area, kneel down, aimed his 'plastic bullet' gun and fire. Brian was struck in the head and died six days later on the 10th October. No soldier has ever been charged in connection with his death.

Location: Norglen Rd
Distance from City Hall: 6.1 km/3.8 miles.
Walking Time: 79 mins
GPS: N 54° 35. 275′ W 5° 59. 446′

Super Heroes

The Super Heroes of the Marvel and DC comic inspired movies are featured on this wall at the Sliabh Dubh estate on Belfast's Springfield Road. The larger than life Characters of Captain America, the Incredible Hulk, Ironman and

Spiderman; along with Wonder Woman and others can be seen systematically smashing through the wall. The mural, painted in October 2013, attracts the attention of young and old and it is not uncommon for local people, and visitors alike to be photographed along with their favourite heroes.

Location: Springfield Road
Distance from City Hall: 5.6 km/3.5 miles.
Walking Time: 73 mins
GPS: N 54° 35. 834´ W 5° 58. 746´

The Battle of Antrim

In 1798, taking their inspiration from the American revolution of 1776 and the French Revolution of 1789, the society of United Irishmen sought to establish Irish political and economic sovereignty. The first actions of the United Irishmen Rebellion took place in Dublin in May 1798, to be followed by the rest of the country. The North, under the leadership of Henry Joy McCracken, Adjutant General of the Army of the Ulster and a member of one of the most prominent Presbyterian families in Belfast, took to the field in support of their southern comrades.

On the 7th June 1798, after some successes in capturing surrounding towns, their forces, although numerically superior, were, in the face of artillery and cavalry, and coupled with confusion, defeated at Antrim. McCracken initially escaped but was later captured, court-martialled and sentenced to death. On the 17th June 1798 he was executed by public hanging at Cornmarket in Belfast's town centre. The mural, located outside

Moyard House on Belfast's Glen Road, which is home to the Roddy McCorley Society, commemorates the United Irishmen by depicting the scene at The Battle of Antrim. The Society, which is named after Roddy McCorley, who himself was a member of the United Irishmen and took part in the rising in Antrim. McCorley was captured and after being placed on trial, was executed on the gallows at Toome.

Function rooms in the club, which are open to the public, have been named after patriots from 1798. The grounds of Moyard House also contain monuments to IRA members who have died on Active Service, Hunger Strikers, United Irishmen and a Memorial Garden dedicated solely to women political activists. The society also maintains their own museum which has an impressive collection of artefacts connected with the Irish Republicanism.

Location: Glen Road/Moyard House
Distance from City Hall: 6.6 km/4.1 miles.
Walking Time: 87 mins
GPS: N 54° 34. 648´ W 6° 00. 810´

McGurk's Bar

Located beneath the West Link motorway, on the support of a flyover is a mural of a small family run pub, with the publican standing at his door. The pub is gone, replaced by a memorial cross and plaques which tell of how a bomb was detonated there by members of the Ulster Volunteer Force. The attack, which took place on 4th December 1971, claimed the lives of fifteen local people, including the publican's wife and daughter. Seventeen others were injured. All the victims came from the Catholic community and the bar was targeted for that reason alone. Despite evidence to the contrary, the official line promoted in the press was that the IRA was responsible for the attack and that the victims were in some way guilty. For more than forty years, family members backed by the local community have demanded justice.

Location: North Queen Street /Great George Street
Distance from City Hall: 1.2 km/.8 miles.
Walking Time: 15 mins
GPS: N 54° 36. 435′ W 5° 56. 818′

New Lodge Six

During the night of the 3rd and 4th of February 1973 loyalist gunmen carried out random, drive by shootings in the New Lodge Road area of Belfast. British soldiers, who were positioned in high rise flats, also opened fire on the community. In total six unarmed men were killed and several others were wounded. The victims, known as the 'New Lodge Six,' were Brendan Maguire, John Loughran and Ambrose Hardy and three IRA members; Jim McCann, Jim Sloan, and Tony Campbell. The findings from a community Inquiry into the shootings states they were not properly investigated and makes the call for justice. This mural was unveiled on the 40th anniversary of the shootings.

Location: New Lodge Road/Donore Court
Distance from City Hall: 2 km/1.3 miles.
Walking Time: 26 mins
GPS: N 54° 36. 718´ W 5° 56. 086´

The Belfast Blitz

When the German Luftwaffe bombed Belfast on the night of Easter Sunday 16th April 1941, they attacked a city, which, although it had a prominent role in the production of war materials, was poorly prepared for war. Only 200 public air rain shelters had been built and a small proportion of the population evacuated. The precise number of those killed that night will never be known but it has been estimated that 900 people were killed and approximately 1,700 were injured. The Belfast Blitz mural, which captures the scene that night, is located in Hogarth Street, in Tigers Bay and which itself, saw many casualties. The mural is dedicated to the 115 people from the area who lost their lives.

Location: Hogarth Street
Distance from City Hall: 2.3 km/1.4 miles.
Walking Time: 29 mins
GPS: N 54° 36. 859´ W 5° 55. 847´

Belfast 1912 - 1918

This mural focuses on the years 1912 -1918 and shows images of events which were happening locally and on the battlefield during the First World War. Images of women welders highlight the changing role of women during the War yearsl, while another shows Belfast shipyard workers on strike for a fair wartime wage in 1917. Elsewhere soldiers are tasked to make crosses to mark the graves of the dead while a bugler playing the Last Post.

A plaque below the mural contains a quote from poem Aftermath by Siegfried Sassoon:

'But the past is just the same, - and War's a bloody game…
Have you forgotten yet? Look down, and swear by the slain
of the War that you'll never forget'.

Location: Mervue Street
Distance from City Hall: 2.3 km/1.4 miles.
Walking Time: 29 mins
GPS: N 54° 36. 878´ W 5° 55. 842´

Black Taxis

Black Taxis have been a feature of Belfast life since the early 1970's when bus services to nationalist areas were frequently withdrawn in response to the on-going conflict. This withdrawal left many people disadvantaged. Adults had difficulty going to and from work, while parents worried about their children travelling to school and home. Local people, recognising the problem, found their solution in the Black Taxi, They travelled to England and purchased old vehicles and set up a community based, transport system. This mural depicts events in the life of Black Taxis; drivers and passengers stopped searched by British Soldiers, the Hunger Strikes, festivals, riots and sectarian attacks. In total eight Black Taxi drivers were killed whilst in the service of their community.

Location: Ardoyne Avenue
Distance from City Hall: 3.8 km/2.4 miles.
Walking Time: 50 mins
GPS: N 54° 36. 894´ W 5° 57. 357´

Racism and Sectarianism

The case of Stephen Lawrence who, in 1993, was killed in a racially motivated attack in England and resulted in an inquiry which concluded that the Metropolitan Police was "institutionally racist," is compared with that of Portadown man, Robert Hamill. Robert Hamill, a Catholic father of three, was beaten unconscious by a loyalist gang in 1987 as he walked through Portadown after an evening out with friends. Robert never regained consciousness and died eleven days later. The attack happened in full view of RUC personnel in a Land Rover but no one intervened to save him.

Location: Brompton Park
Distance from City Hall: 3.7 km/2.3 miles.
Walking Time: 48 mins
GPS: N 54° 36. 921´ W 5° 57. 416´

Sandy Row

Sandy Row, like so many other areas of Belfast has saw many changes over the past one hundred years. Redevelopment has seen aspects of the old neighbourhood being swept away and with it many of its local personalities and characters displaced and familiar sights gone. This mural, or rather the series of murals which stretch along Stroud Street, laments many of the changes to the area and captures the spirit of the community. Sections of the mural have been reproduced from photographs dating back to 1907 and show both the streets and the characters who lived there. Images of local people such as James Johnston, the opera singing butcher appear alongside fruit sellers, tram workers and lamplighters as well as sporting legends of the past and present.

The imagination and innovation of children who could create a play park out of any environment is also celebrated in the mural. Often children, using a piece of rope and a street lamp, would make an effective but somewhat dangerous

swing on which they could play. The mural artist's clever use of the physical environment adds an interesting and unusual quality to the mural, as can be seen by the painting of children close to a modern street lamp. The same effect of merging the physical environment with the mural is employed in the drawing of a man 'Clocking on' for work which has been positioned beside a parking ticket machine.

Location: Stroud Street
Distance from City Hall: 1.2 km/0.7 miles.
Walking Time: 15 mins
GPS: N 54° 35. 362´ W 5° 56. 086´

William of Orange

William of Orange, continues to be a popular subject for murals in loyalist areas of Belfast. Indeed it is reported that the first such mural was painted in 1908 on Belfast's Beersbridge Road. The above mural, located at Shankill Parade, depicts William crossing the River Boyne in 1690. The Battle of the Boyne is considered to be the decisive battle between the Catholic King James and the Protestant King William for the throne of England. The battle, while also being part of a greater European power struggle, in Ireland it established Protestant ascendancy over Catholics . Ironically, the Catholic pope in 1690, Pope Alexander VIII was himself an ally of William. The victory over James is celebrated by the Protestant Orange Order each year on the 12th July.

Location: Sandy Row/Linfield Road
Distance from City Hall: 900 m/ 0.5 miles.
Walking Time: 11 mins
GPS: N 54° 36. 310´ W 5° 56. 534´

East Belfast Historical and Cultural Society

Thorndyke Street in East Belfast is the location of a mural, commissioned by the East Belfast Historical and Cultural Society, which takes the form of a set of reliefs which focus on significant events in local history. Taking as its starting point the 'Plantation of Ulster', the mural with imagery and accompanying text, relates, through unionist eyes, the Seige of Derry, the founding of the Orange Order and the Ulster Covenant. Other themes illustrated are the Battle of the Somme, the Blitz, the IRA and 'Loyalty Betrayed' which focuses on the Disbandment of the B Specials and Ulster Defence Regiment. The mural featured above recalls the Ulster Workers Council strike of 1974 and the collapse of the power sharing Executive.

Location: Thorndyke Street
Distance from City Hall: 2.2 km/1.4 miles.
Walking Time: 28 mins
GPS: N 54° 35. 715´ W 5° 54. 037´

Ship of Dreams

A small plaque to the side of the 'Ship of Dreams' mural states that 'The Titanic was a ship of dreams, its reality and design began in the mind dream of one man, thousands of others helped create and rivet metal into myth. This artwork celebrates the reality of dreams caught forever within one single voyage' The mural, located in east Belfast, where the ship was built, carries the images of the ship itself as it left Belfast, its captain, Edward Smyth, designer Thomas Andrews and Jack Phillips its wireless operator. Included also are the co-ordinates of its last known location 41°46n, 50°14w. On the 14th April 1912, the Titanic was carrying 2,223 passengers and crew, of these 1,517 perished, only 706 survived.

Location: Newtownards Road
Distance from City Hall: 1.5 km/.9 miles.
Walking Time: 19 mins
GPS: N 54° 36. 018´ W 5° 54. 451´

Ulster's Past Defenders

In the shadow of the Harland and Wolf cranes Ulster's Past Defenders mural stretches along the lower section of the Newtownards Road and highlights the role of official state forces and paramilitary groups in the establishment and defence of the northern state. Sections of the mural focus on the Ulster Special Constabulary and the Ulster Defence Regiment as well as the Ulster Defence Association and Ulster Freedom Fighters.

The Ulster Special Constabulary, or as they were commonly known the 'B' Specials were a part time force established in October 1920. The force was almost exclusively Protestant in make up and at its formation had as many as 19,000 members. While supported by the unionist community they were viewed by nationalists as being a sectarian force. The organisation was disbanded in 1970 and was replaced by the Ulster Defence Regiment (UDR).

Location: Newtownards Road
Distance from City Hall: 2 km/1.2 miles.
Walking Time: 25 mins
GPS: N 54° 35. 971′ W 5° 54. 217′

36th Ulster Division

The 36th Ulster Division which was formed in September 1914 and was made up by members of the Ulster Volunteer Force, a Protestant militia which had been created in 1912, in order to resist Home Rule for Ireland. The Division is best known for its participation in action on the Western Front at the Battle of the Somme. It was there, at Thiepval Wood, on the 1st July 1916, that the Division suffered over 5,000 casualties, of which 2,069 were fatal. Of the nine Victoria Crosses awarded that day three were won by members of the 36th Ulster Division. William McFadzean and Eric Bell were both posthumously awarded the VC, while its third winner, Robert Quigg, survived the carnage of the Somme.

Location: Newtownards Road/St Leonards Crescent
Distance from City Hall: 1.3km/1.3 miles.
Walking Time: 26 mins
GPS: N 54° 35. 941´ W 5° 53. 983´

APRIL 14, 1912.

Titanic

The RMS Titanic, built in Belfast for the White Star Line, has, since it struck an iceberg off the coast of Newfoundland, passed into legend. Carrying 2,223 men, women and children, taking many of them to what was to be a new life in America. Titanic set to sea from Southampton on 10th April 1912, four days later, her maiden voyage ended and with it the lives of 1,517 passengers and crew. Only 706 men, women and children survived the disaster. This mural at Dee Street, once the route which workers took on their way to the Harland & Wolfe shipyard where the ship was built, shows the iconic ship set against a backdrop of familiar East Belfast sights.

Location: Newtownards Road/Dee Street
Distance from City Hall: 2.3 km/1.4 miles.
Walking Time: 29 mins
GPS: N 54° 35. 922′   W 5° 53. 835′

Narnia

Irish author, poet and academic C.S. Lewis was born in Belfast in 1896. He grew up in the east of the city. Although Lewis left Belfast at an early age he maintained a fondness for the City and country, which it has been said inspired his classic series 'The Chronicles of Narnia'. The Narnia mural at Pansy Street draws heavily on the film adaptation of his books. Lewis's stature has grown since his death in 1963, and of his 30 published works, the Narnia books have proven to be most popular with an estimated 100 million books being sold worldwide and translated into thirty languages.

Location: Dee St/Pansy St
Distance from City Hall: 2.6 km/1.6 miles.
Walking Time: 32 mins
GPS: N 54° 36. 025´   W 5° 53. 802´

Throughout Belfast there are many locations which are associated with the Lewis family and the Narnia Chronicles. Campbell College, located in the east of the city is thought to be the location of an old gas lamp which featured prominently in the books and films.   However, one of the most popular sites is located at Holywood Arches library on the Holywood Road (approximately ten minutes walking time from the mural).

Situated outside the Library is a life size statue of Lewis, as the character of Digory Kirke, the narrator of the Chronicles of Narnia, entering the magical wardrobe. The sculpture was created by artist Ross Wilson.

Years of Sacrifice

The Carlingford Street mural painted in November 2013 and which features the Nissen huts of Long Kesh prison, along with the UVF emblem and armed men. The mural is dedicated to four members of the loyalist Ulster Volunteer Force who were killed during the conflict. Painted just a short distance from a police barracks, the mural attracted criticism when it became known that it was linked to the UVF, which in previous the weeks had shot a local woman six times. As a result of the criticism, the mural was modified, masked UVF men were replaced by images of armed members of the Ulster Volunteer Force which fought as part of the 36th Ulster Division during the First World War.

Location: Carlingford Street/Ardenvohr Street:
Distance from City Hall: 2.7 km/1.6 miles.
Walking Time: 33 mins
GPS: N 54° 35. 326´ W 5° 54. 223´

'The Great War'

The First World War, on a global basis cost the lives of more than nine million men, women and children. Over 200,000 Irishmen fought in the war with almost 30,000 of them being killed. Over 11,000 of these came from the North. This mural focuses on combatants who hailed from the Sydenham area of Belfast; a small plaque lists their names. Prominence is also give to figures from the 1914-1918 period, The Unionist politician Lord Edward Carson and Private William McFadzean. McFadzean, aged 20 from Lurgan in County Armagh, was posthumously awarded the Victoria Cross for bravery, when, becoming aware that safety pins on two hand grenades had become dislodged, he threw himself on top of them. Using his body as a shield he saved the lives of his comrades.

Location: Inverary Drive/Station Road, Sydenham
Distance from City Hall: 2.3 km/1.4 miles.
Walking Time: 29 mins
GPS: N 54° 35. 922´ W 5° 53. 835´

The Markets

Located close to Belfast city centre, the Markets area is one of Belfast's oldest communities and takes its name from the various markets which flourished there as the city developed. All of these open aired markets are now gone, however the area is the location of Belfast's only covered Market, St George's which was built in 1890. A short distance from the market, at Friendly Way, is a mural which remembers seven members of the IRA, who came from the local community and who lost their lives in the conflict. The centre piece of the mural shows an IRA Active Service Unit, armed with a Russian made RPG7 rocket launcher.

Location: Friendly Way
Distance from City Hall: 1.1 km/.7 miles.
Walking Time: 13 mins
GPS: N 54° 35. 695´ W 5° 55. 221´

Sean Martin

On the 25th April 1940, IRA member Sean Martin was instructing his comrades in the use of hand grenades when he noticed that a grenade was faulty and was about to explode. The room was crowded, children were playing outside in the street and the grenade couldn't be safely disposed of. Selflessly he threw his body on to the exploding grenade thereby saving the lives of those around him. This mural remembers his actions. Written in Irish on the mural are the words: 'Grádh níos fearr ní raibh ag duine na a bheo a thabhairt ar son a chomrádaithe,' 'No greater love has a man than to lay down his life for his comrades.'

Location: Beechfield Street
Distance from City Hall: 1.8 km/1.1 miles.
Walking Time: 23 mins
GPS: N 54° 35. 877′ W 5° 54. 528′

Charlie Monahan

During the preparations for the 1916 Rising, Charlie Monahan, from Belfast, a member of the Irish Volunteers, along with two comrades, was tasked with capturing a wireless station in County Kerry so weapons could be landed at Banna Strand. In bad weather their vehicle crashed into a river and all three men died. A German ship 'The Aud' which was carrying 20,000 rifles and one million rounds of ammunition for the Rising, was intercepted and then scuttled. Roger Casement who had procured the weapons was later hanged in Pentonville Prison in England on the 3rd August 1916 for his role in the gun running. Charlie Monahan was the first republican from the North to lose his life during the Rising.

Location: Mountpottinger Road
Distance from City Hall: 1.7 km/1 miles.
Walking Time: 21 mins
GPS: N 54° 35. 896´ W 5° 54. 582´

Places of Interest

Milltown Cemetery

The first burials took place in Milltown Cemetery in 1869 when it superseded Friars Bush as the primary Catholic cemetery in the Belfast area. Whereas the City Cemetery can trace the history of industrial Belfast, Milltown is the burial ground for Belfast's nationalist community. Almost 500,000 of the city's citizens are buried on the 62 acre site. 80,000 of these, many of whom were victims of the pan endemic flu of 1919, are buried in unmarked graves in the cemetery's poor ground. Also located in the cemetery are the graves of more than 100 British soldiers who died during the first and second world wars. Milltown is perhaps best known for the large number of Republican graves and monuments located there and in particular it is where Bobby Sands, Joe McDonnell and Kieran Doherty, who died on Hunger Strike are buried.

Location: Falls Road
Distance from City Hall: 4.1 km/2.5miles.
Walking Time: 52 mins
GPS: N 54° 35. 061´ W 5° 58. 683´

City Cemetery

Cemeteries tell the history of their communities and the City Cemetery is no different; the divisions of class and religion are apparent. Located in West Belfast, the City Cemetery would be considered to be a Protestant cemetery with a unionist history. Impressive tombs for the city's industrialists and shipbuilders dominate the cemetery and dwarf the graves of working class protestants. The cemetery was initially designed to have Catholic, Protestant and Jewish sections; graves were categorised according to price, location and religious belief. Even separate entrances were created for the city's dead. This division was taken even further, with the construction of a nine foot deep underground wall which would also separate the dead. The absurdity of this idea appears to have been lost on the planners and the scheme was only abandoned after approximately 100 yards of the wall was constructed.

Location: Falls Road
Distance from City Hall: 3.3 km/2.1 miles.
Walking Time: 43 mins
GPS: N 54° 35. 308´   W 5° 58. 203´

Peace Walls

Located throughout the city, are the so called 'Peace Walls;' interfaces which have been created between Republican and Unionist areas. There are no exact statistics relating to the number of these walls, but some estimates state that there are approximately 48 throughout the Six Counties. The vast majority of these walls, some of which stand more than 30 feet high, are in Belfast and if connected together would stretch for almost 13 miles. Examples of these interfaces can be seen at various locations throughout the city however one of the worst examples can be seen at Cupar Way (between North Howard Street and Lanark Way.

Location: Cupar Way
Distance from City Hall: 1.6 km/1.1 miles.
Walking Time: 21 mins
GPS: N 54° 36. 073´   W 5° 57. 725´

Crumlin Road Gaol

Belfast Prison, designed by architect Charles Lanyon was built between 1843 and 1845. Its design was based on London's Pentonville Prison. Four wings radiating from a central 'Circle' area, ensured that each wing could be observed from a central point. In 1852 a tunnel linking the courthouse to the gaol was constructed under the Crumlin Road to facilitate the secure transport of prisoners to court. This tunnel was used up until the gaol eventually closed. In the 1970's, the prison population explode and it has been estimated that as many as 25,000 political prisoners were held at Crumlin Road. Conflict and prison protests were daily occurrence in the prison. By the time the prison closed its doors in March 1996 it had witnessed the imprisonment of suffragettes and child prisoners, internment, escapes and executions. Tours of the prison are available seven days a week: 10.00am to 4.30pm. Enquiries Tel: 028 90741500

Location:Crumlin Road
Distance from City Hall: 1.8 km/1.1 miles.
Walking Time: 24 mins
GPS: N 54° 36. 521´ W 5° 56. 538´

Eileen Hickey Museum

The Eileen Hickey, Republican History Museum, opened in 2006 and is located in Conway Mill. This small, but comprehensive museum offers the visitor an insight into the conflict, both inside and outside of the prisons. Whilst the museum's main focus is on republicanism, there are on display there many examples of unionist political artefacts. The museum holds a large selection of prison crafts, photographs and posters. The permanent exhibitions are being continually added and the staff are more than willing to give an insight into any of the artefacts on display. The museum also has a computerised information centre and research library.

Open: - Tuesday to Saturday 10.00am to 2.00pm
Admission is free.

Location: Conway St
Distance from City Hall: 1.7 km/1.1 miles.
Walking Time: 22 mins
GPS: N 54° 35. 957′ W 5° 57. 079′

Belfast Mural Guide GPS Locations

Mural	Location	GPS
Finn McCool	King St	N 54° 35. 997' W 5° 56. 079'
Duke of York	Commercial Ct	N 54° 36. 099' W 5° 55. 633'
John Peel	Commercial Ct/Donegal St	N 54° 36. 093' W 5° 55. 708'
Jim Larkin	Donegal St Pl	N 54° 36. 120' W 5° 55. 681'
Dance By Candlelight	Exchange Pl/Hill St	N 54° 36. 165' W 5° 55. 968'
Pound Loney	Durham Street	N 54° 35. 880' W 5° 55. 337'
Welcome to West Belfast	Divis St	N 54° 35. 975' W 5° 56. 791'
One Race, One Love, One World	Divis St/Divis Tower	N 54° 35. 012' W 5° 56. 531'
Basque Mural	Divis St	N 54° 35. 989' W 5° 56. 728'
Free All Political Prisoners	Divis St	N 54° 35. 988' W 5° 56. 727'
Free Leonard Peltier	Divis St	N 54° 35. 988' W 5° 56. 727'
Hungerstrike Mural	Divis St	N 54° 35. 989' W 5° 56. 728'
G.P.O.	Divis St	N 54° 35. 988' W 5° 56. 731'
Women of Easter 1916	Divis St	N 54° 35. 987' W 5° 56. 736'
Local IRA Volunteers	Divis St	N 54° 35. 987' W 5° 56. 736'
Easter Rising 1916	Divis St	N 54° 35. 975' W 5° 56. 791'

Mural	Location	GPS
Mandela, Friend of Ireland	Northumberland St	N 54° 35. 987' W 5° 56. 736'
Francis Hughes	Northumberland St	N 54° 35. 991' W 5° 56. 802'
IRSP	Northumberland St	N 54° 35. 995' W 5° 56. 806'
International Brigade	Northumberland St	N 54° 36. 003' W 5° 56. 812'
Amnesty International	Northumberland St	N 54° 36. 010' W 5° 56. 817'
Salvador Allende	Northumberland St	N 54° 36. 037' W 5° 56. 836'
Freedom for Ocalan	Northumberland St	N 54° 36. 016' W 5° 56. 821'
Pobal: Irish Language	Northumberland St	N 54° 36. 010' W 5° 56. 817'
Arising from the Troubles	Northumberland St	N 54° 36. 014' W 5° 56. 820'
End Sectarianism	Northumberland St	N 54° 36. 019' W 5° 56. 823'
Climate Change	Northumberland St	N 54° 36. 018' W 5° 56. 825'
Palestinian Solidarity	Northumberland St	N 54° 36. 018' W 5° 56. 823'
Fredrick Douglas	Northumberland St	N 54° 36. 037' W 5° 56. 836'
Welcome to the Shankill	Northumberland St	N 54° 36. 077' W 5° 56. 833'
Demand Dignity	Northumberland St	N 54° 36. 089' W 5° 56. 832'
Battle of Britain	Northumberland St/Beverley St	N 54° 36. 085' W 5° 56. 833'
Polish 305 Squadron	Northumberland St/Beverley St	N 54° 36. 091' W 5° 56. 809'
Suicide Awareness	Divis St/Albert St	N 54° 35. 965' W 5° 56. 785'
'D' Company Mural	Falls Rd	N 54° 35. 927' W 5° 57. 009'
Mother Jones	North Howard St	N 54° 36. 009' W 5° 56. 980'
Republican History Museum	Conway St	N 54° 35. 957' W 5° 57. 079'

Mural

Mural	Location	GPS	
Archbishop Romero	Conway St/Conway Link	N 54° 35. 948'	W 5° 57. 088'
Hunger Strikers	Falls Rd/Falls Library	N 54° 35. 889'	W 5° 57. 140'
Bobby Sands Mural	Falls Rd/Savastopol St	N 54° 35. 872'	W 5° 57. 163'
Oige_na_Bhfal	Ross Rd/Sultan Way	N 54° 35. 851'	W 5° 56. 799'
Mol na nÓige	Roumania Rise	N 54° 35. 900'	W 5° 56. 736'
Muhammad Ali	Roumania Rise	N 54° 35. 886'	W 5° 56. 785'
Immacualta Boxing Club	Roumania Rise	N 54° 35. 881'	W 5° 56. 805'
Seán MacDiarmada	Clonard Street	N54° 35. 835'	W 5° 57. 240'
Easter Rising 1916-2016	Falls Rd/McQuillan St	N 54° 35. 778'	W 5° 57. 303'
August '69: Never Again	Bombay St	N 54° 36. 067'	W 5° 57. 473'
Boxing mural	Cavendish St/Violet St	N 54° 35. 716'	W 5° 57. 427'
Ireland 1845/Syria 2015	Cavendish St/Crocus St	N 54° 35. 734'	W 5° 57. 465'
Gibraltar	Cavendish St/Hawthorne St	N 54° 35. 736'	W 5° 57. 507'
Cumann na mBan	Cavendish St/Hawthorne St	N 54° 35. 736'	W 5° 57. 507'
Ulster's Defender, Past & Present	High Green/Highcairn Drive	N 54° 36. 164'	W 5° 58. 584'
UDA	Highcairn Drive	N 54° 35. 953'	W 5° 58. 546'
UFF	Highcairn Drive	N 54° 35. 953'	W 5° 58. 546'
Orange Order	Cambrai Street	N 54° 36. 439'	W 5° 57. 552'
Women through the Ages	Enfield St/Cambrai St	N 54° 36. 453'	W 5° 57. 567'
James Buchanan 15th US President	Woodvale Rd/Ainsworth St	N 54° 36. 384'	W 5° 57. 672'
Ernest 'Duke' Elliott	Ohio St/Colombia St	N 54° 36. 628'	W 5° 57. 520'

83

Mural

Mural	Location	GPS
Brian Robinson	Disraeli St/Enfield Pde	N 54° 36. 549′ W 5° 57. 662′
Trevor King	Disraeli St/Enfield St	N 54° 36. 539′ W 5° 57. 669′
Sam Rockett	Disraeli St/Enfield Dr	N 54° 36. 533′ W 5° 57. 673′
Brian Robinson	Disraeli St/Enfield Pde	N 54° 36. 511′ W 5° 57. 690′
Woodvale Defence Association	Disraeli St/Enfield St	N 54° 36. 486′ W 5° 57. 709′
Red Hand Commandos	Shankill Rd/Glenwood St	N 54° 36. 264′ W 5° 57. 373′
UVF	Shankill Rd/Glenwood St	N 54° 36. 264′ W 5° 57. 373′
UVF 'C' Company	Shankill Rd/1 Carnan St	N 54° 36. 261′ W 5° 57. 249′
Hugh Smyth	Shankill Rd/Canmore St	N 54° 36. 247′ W 5° 57. 192′
Ulster Tower	Shankill Rd/Conway St	N 54° 36. 452′ W 5° 56. 715′
UVF Battle of the Somme	Northland St/Conway St	N 54° 36. 169′ W 5° 57. 094′
Ulster Covanant/ Somme	Shankill Rd/Rex Bar	N 54° 36. 241′ W 5° 57. 000′
UVF Preparing to Bear Arms	Shankill Rd/Speirs Pl	N 54° 36. 246′ W 5° 57. 984′
Queen/Flags/ Ulster to England	Shankill Rd/Crimea St	N 54° 36. 259′ W 5° 56. 953′
Thiepval	Shankill Rd/ Iceland	N 54° 36. 237′ W 5° 56. 890′
30 years of slaughter	Shankill Rd/ Iceland	N 54° 36. 288′ W 5° 56. 856′
Titanic/Shipyards	Shankill Rd/ Downing St	N 54° 36. 247′ W 5° 56. 777′
VE Day	Dover Pl	N 54° 36. 194′ W 5° 56. 634′
Percy Street Belfast Blitz	Dover Pl	N 54° 36. 194′ W 5° 56. 624′
Sons & Fathers Enlist	Dover Pl	N 54° 36. 192′ W 5° 56. 599′
Welcome to the Shankill	Peters Hill/Gardiner St	N 54° 36. 180′ W 5° 56. 191′

Mural	Location	GPS
Original Shankill	Peters Hill	N 54° 36. 205' W 5° 56. 396'
A-Z History of the Shankill	North Boundary St	N 54° 36. 278' W 5° 56. 394'
William of Orange	Shankill Pde	N 54° 36. 310' W 5° 56. 534'
Jackie Coulter	Shankill Pde	N 54° 36. 311' W 5° 56. 473'
Bucky McCullough	Hopewell Cres	N 54° 36. 358' W 5° 56. 396'
Gold Rush of '69	Hopewell Cres	N 54° 36. 358' W 5° 56. 396'
Stevie 'Topgun' McKeague	Hopewell Cres	N 54° 36. 365' W 5° 56. 534'
The Women's Quilt	Hopewell Cres	N 54° 36. 364' W 5° 56. 512'
Angels	Hopewell Cres	N 54° 36. 358' W 5° 56. 396'
Summer of '69	Hopewell Ave	N 54° 36. 452' W 5° 56. 715'
Red Hand Commandos	Hopewell Ave	N 54° 36. 452' W 5° 56. 715'
Life in Malvern St School	Hopewell Ave	N 54° 36. 486' W 5° 56. 715'
Never Doubt	Hopewell Ave	N 54° 36. 437' W 5° 56. 391'
Nothing About Us, Without Us	Malvern Way/Shankill Pde	N 54° 36. 288' W 5° 56. 560'
Stop Calling me Resilient	Boundary Way	N 54° 36. 243' W 5° 56. 488'
Sport	Springfield Cr/Springfield Rd	N 54° 35. 415' W 5° 55. 622'
Kashmir Bar	Springfield Cr/Springfield Rd	N 54° 35. 415' W 5° 55. 622'
Clonard	Springfield Dr/Springfield Rd	N 54° 35. 400' W 5° 55. 618'
Suicide Awareness	Falls Rd/Shiels St	N 54° 35. 547' W 5° 57. 662'
Advocacy for the Irish Language	Falls Rd/Brighton St	N 54° 35. 549' W 5° 57. 704'
Suicide Awareness	Falls Rd/Fallswater St	N 54° 35. 530' W 5° 57. 689'

Mural	Location	GPS
Sean Maguire	Falls Rd/Iveagh Pde	N 54° 35. 529' W 5° 57. 733'
Victims of Plastic Bullets	Falls Rd/Islandbawn St	N 54° 35. 529' W 5° 57. 733'
Easter Rising 1916	Falls Rd/Beechmount Ave	N 54° 35. 510' W 5° 57. 821'
National Graves Association	Falls Rd/Beechmount Ave	N 54° 35. 510' W 5° 57. 821'
Freedom of Women	Falls Rd/Beechmount Ave	N 54° 35. 510' W 5° 57. 821'
Hunger Strike Mural	Beechmount Ave/Clowney St	N 54° 35. 551' W 5° 57. 829'
Freedom for Catalonia Mural	Beechmount Ave/Clowney St	N 54° 35. 551' W 5° 57. 829'
Viva Palestine	Beechmount Ave	N 54° 35. 570' W 5° 57. 812'
Free All Basque Political Prisoners	Beechmount Ave	N 54° 35. 654' W 5° 57. 761'
Sankara	Beechmount Ave	N 54° 35. 670' W 5° 57. 732'
Collusion Wall	Beechmount Ave	N 54° 35. 685' W 5° 57. 711'
One Community, One World	Beechmount Ave	N 54° 35. 616' W 5° 57. 796'
Stop, Look, Listen	Beechmount Ave	N 54° 35. 616' W 5° 57. 796'
Famine	Oakman St	N 54° 35. 699' W 5° 57. 889'
Pat Finucane	Falls Rd/Beechmount Dr	N 54° 35. 506' W 5° 57. 857'
You'll Never Walk Alone	Ballymurphy St/Beechmount St	N 54° 35. 650' W 5° 57. 876'
We Only Want The Earth	Falls Rd/Rockmount Street	N 54° 35. 338' W 5° 58. 177'
Women in Struggle	Falls Rd/Rockmount St	N 54° 35. 338' W 5° 58. 177'
The First Blanketman	Falls Rd/Rockville St	N 54° 35. 365' W 5° 58. 143'
Portraits of Hunger Strikers	Falls Rd/Rockmore Rd	N 54° 35. 356' W 5° 58. 154'
Patrick O'Connell	Whiterock Rd/Falls Road	N 54° 35. 319' W 5° 58. 194'

Mural	Location	GPS
Francis Liggett/Paddy Brady	Donegall Rd/St James Cres	N 54° 35. 304' W 5° 57. 883'
Belfast Celtic	St James Rd/St Katherines Rd	N 54° 35. 227' W 5° 57. 925'
Cliftonville & Celtic	St James Rd/St Katherines Rd	N 54° 35. 227' W 5° 57. 925'
James Connolly	Falls Rd/Clondara St	N 54° 35. 269' W 5° 58. 208'
From Bullet to Ballot	Falls Rd/Hugo St	N 54° 35. 305' W 5° 58. 205'
Portraits of Hunger Strikers	Falls Rd/Rockmore Rd	N 54° 35. 356' W 5° 58. 154'
Francis Liggett/Paddy Brady	Donegall Rd/St James Cres	N 54° 35. 304' W 5° 57. 883'
Belfast Celtic	St James Rd/St Katherines Rd	N 54° 35. 227' W 5° 57. 925'
Cliftonville & Celtic	St James Rd/St Katherines Rd	N 54° 35. 227' W 5° 57. 925'
Free All Basque Political Prisoners	Falls Rd/Glen Rd	N 54° 35. 040' W 5° 58. 773'
The Birth of the Republic	Falls Rd	N 54° 34. 935' W 5° 58. 774'
Kieran Doherty	Andersontown Rd/Slemish Way	N 54° 34. 458' W 5° 59. 160'
1916 – 2016, Unbowed, Unbroken	South Link	N54° 34. 523' W 5° 59. 335
Patsy O'Hara	Shaws Rd	N 54° 34. 544' W 6° 00. 348'
Hurling	Shaws Rd	N 54° 34. 522' W 6° 00. 321'
Battle of Antrim	Glen Rd/ Roddy McCorlai Society	N 54° 34. 648' W 6° 00. 810'
The Great Hunger	Lenadoon Ave	N 54° 34. 286' W 6° 00. 613'
Joe McDonnell	Lenadoon Ave	N 54° 34. 259' W 6° 00. 582'
Lenadoon Roll of Honour	Lenadoon Ave	N 54° 34. 536' W 6° 00. 713'
Gaelic Games	Lenadoon Ave	N 54° 34. 536' W 6° 00. 713'
Environment	Lenadoon Ave	N 54° 34. 536' W 6° 00. 713'
Women in Struggle	Lenadoon Ave/Dungloe Cres	N 54° 34. 552' W 6° 00. 677'

Mural	Location	GPS
Julie Livingstone	Glenveagh Dr	N 54° 34. 521' W 6° 01. 278'
Lenadoon	Carrigart Ave	N 54° 34. 364' W 6° 01. 120'
Anti Racism World Cup	Carrigart Ave	N 54° 34. 364' W 6° 01. 120'
Joe McDonnell	Suffolk Rd	N 54° 34. 420' W 6° 01. 288'
Donegal Celtic	Suffolk Rd	N 54° 34. 433' W 6° 01. 288'
Estát Ghleann Collain	Glencolin Way	N 54° 34. 601' W 6° 00. 878'
Carol Ann Kelly	Aspen Pk	N 54° 33. 252' W 6° 01. 096'
Volunteers of Óglaigh na hÉireann	Almond Dr	N 54° 33. 091' W 6° 01. 590'
Death of Cúchulain	Glenbawn Ave	N 54° 33. 480' W 6° 02. 026'
Welcome to Glenbawn	Glenbawn Ave	N 54° 33. 548' W 6° 02. 109'
In Memory of the Hunger Strikers	Glenwood Dr	N 54° 33. 618' W 6° 01. 727'
Joe Cahill	Brittons Pde/Beechview Pk	N 54° 35. 467' W 5° 58. 429'
Ballymurphy Republicans	Divismore Cres	N 54° 35. 735' W 5° 59. 082'
Cumann na mBan	Ballymurphy Rd	N 54° 35. 545' W 5° 58. 840'
Óglaigh na h-Éireann	Glenalina Rd	N 54° 35. 616' W 5° 59. 014'
Tommy Tolan	Ballymurphy Cres	N 54° 35. 688' W 5° 58. 969'
Jim Bryson	Ballymurphy Rd	N 54° 35. 685' W 5° 58. 829'
Dublin, Easter 1916	Whiterock Rd/Glenalina Rd	N 54° 35. 589' W 5° 59. 097'
IRA Volunteers	Glenalina Rd	N 54° 35. 659' W 5° 58. 993'
Belfast Graves	Glenalina Rd	N 54° 35. 828' W 5° 58. 749'
Internment without Trial	Springhill Ave	N 54° 35. 675' W 5° 59. 010'

Mural

Mural	Location	GPS
Palestine Abú	Springhill Ave	N 54° 35. 675′ W 5° 59. 010′
The Blanket Men	Springhill Ave	N 54° 35. 748′ W 5° 58. 766′
Ballymurphy Massacre	Springfield Rd	N 54° 35. 693′ W 5° 59. 210′
IRSP	Springfield Rd	N 54° 35. 684′ W 5° 59. 230′
The Usual Suspects	Springfield Rd	N 54° 35. 716′ W 5° 59. 164′
The Final Salute	Whiterock Rd/Springfield Rd	N 54° 35. 673′ W 5° 59. 256′
Nuada of the Silver Arm	Whiterock Rd	N 54° 35. 673′ W 5° 59. 256′
The Mass Graves of Ireland	Springfield Rd	N 54° 35. 834′ W 5° 58. 746′
Springhill Massacre	Springfield Rd	N 54° 35. 834′ W 5° 58. 746′
Brian Stewart	Norglen Rd	N 54° 35. 275′ W 5° 59. 446′
Super Heroes	Springfield Rd/Sliabh Dubh	N 54° 35. 834′ W 5° 58. 746′
Support Your Mates	Moyard Pde	N 54° 35. 863′ W 5° 59. 188′
They May Kill the Revolutionary	Norglen Pde	N 54° 35. 478′ W 5° 59. 342′
Terry Enright	Gort na Mona GAA Club/Avoca Close	N 54° 35. 347′ W 5° 59. 739′
Its Like a Jungle	Union St	N 54° 36. 108′ W 5° 55. 620′
Long Runs The Fox	Lr North St	N 54° 36. 108′ W 5° 55. 620′
Belfast Phoenix	Lr North St	N 54° 36. 108′ W 5° 55. 620′
Fight or Flight	Lr North St	N 54° 36. 108′ W 5° 55. 620′
Culture Night Mural	Kent St/Union St	N 54° 36. 108′ W 5° 55. 620′
Culture Night Mural	Kent St/Union St	N 54° 36. 108′ W 5° 55. 620′
Culture Night Mural	Kent St	N 54° 36. 189′ W 5° 55. 947′

Mural	Location	GPS	
Culture Night Mural - Monkey	Library St	N 54° 36. 437'	W 5° 56. 391'
Culture Night Mural - Phrases	Donegall St	N 54° 36. 242'	W 5° 55. 852'
Culture Night Mural	William St/Royal Ave	N 54° 36. 116'	W 5° 55. 848'
Culture Night Mural	Church St/North St	N 54° 36. 118'	W 5° 55. 836'
Culture Night Mural	Lr North St	N 54° 36. 067'	W 5° 55. 760'
Culture Night Mural	Lr North St	N 54° 36. 058'	W 5° 55. 742'
Culture Night Mural	High St	N 54° 36. 014'	W 5° 55. 572'
McGurks Bar	North Queen St/Gt Georges St	N 54° 36. 435'	W 5° 56. 818'
New Lodge Six	New Lodge Rd/Donore Ct	N 54° 36. 718'	W 5° 56. 086'
O'Neill/Allsopp Band	New Lodge Rd/Donore Ct	N 54° 36. 718'	W 5° 56. 086'
New Lodge 1900	New Lodge Rd	N 54° 36. 646'	W 5° 55. 852'
Free the POWs	New Lodge Rd/Ludlow Sq	N 54° 36. 636'	W 5° 55. 848'
Aboriginal	New Lodge Rd/Ludlow Sq	N 54° 36. 637'	W 5° 55. 849'
IRA Role of Honour	New Lodge Rd	N 54° 36. 618'	W 5° 55. 814'
New Lodge 2000	New Lodge Rd/New Lodge Pl	N 54° 36. 607'	W 5° 55. 794'
The Great Hunger	New Lodge Rd/North Queen St	N 54° 36. 577'	W 5° 55. 738'
Rosa Parks	Lepper St/Hillman St	N 54° 36. 742'	W 5° 55. 870'
Welcome to Sailortown	Dock St	N 54° 36. 519'	W 5° 55. 202'
Building an Ireland of Equals	Antrim Rd/Oceanic Dr	N 54° 37. 038'	W 5° 56. 269'
Tiger Bay First Flute Band	Hogarth St/Mervue St	N 54° 36. 829'	W 5° 55. 708'
The Belfast Blitz 1941	Hogarth St/Edlingham St	N 54° 36. 859'	W 5° 55. 847'

Mural	Location	GPS
Belfast 1912-1918	Mervue Street	N 54° 36. 878' W 5° 55. 842'
Titanic Workers	Hogarth St/Edlingham St	N 54° 36. 859' W 5°55. 847'
Community, Pride & Culture	North Queen St/Cultra St	N 54° 36. 820' W 5° 55. 566'
Midland Boxing Club	Cultra St	N 54° 36. 819' W 5° 55. 502'
Tigers Bay. Yes to a Better Future	North Queen St	N 54° 36. 841' W 5° 55. 580'
Crusaders	St Vincent St	N 54° 37. 417' W 5° 55. 349'
Titanic Town 1912	St Vincent St	N 54° 37. 423' W 5° 55. 267'
York Road Defence Hall	St Vincent St	N 54° 37. 423' W 5° 55. 267'
HMS Caroline	St Aubyn St	N 54° 37. 404' W 5° 55. 283'
Laughter of Our Children	Newington St/Atlantic Ave	N 54° 36. 968' W 5° 56. 176'
Welcome to Ardoyne	Ardoyne Rd	N 54° 36. 909' W 5° 57. 954'
Easter 1916	Berwick Rd/Brompton Pk	N 54° 36. 921' W 5° 57. 663'
Medugorje	Berwick/Estorial Pk	N 54° 36. 958' W 5° 57. 688'
Cogus	Berwick Rd	N 54° 37. 006' W 5° 57. 720'
Record Breaker	Berwick/ Rd/Farringdon Gds	N 54° 37. 020' W 5° 57. 729'
Fianna	Berwick Rd/Alliance Ave	N 54° 37. 072' W 5° 57. 765'
Ardoyne Festival	Brompton Pk	N 54° 36. 921' W 5° 57. 416'
Racism and Sectarianism	Brompton Pk/Havana Way	N 54° 36. 921' W 5° 57. 416'
Ardoyne Youth Past & Present	Flax Street/Herbert St	N 54° 36. 834' W 5° 57. 441'
Ardoyne Kickhams GAA Club	Ardoyne Ave	N 54° 36. 926' W 5° 57. 387'
Ardoyne Volunteers	Ardoyne Ave/Havana Way	N 54° 36. 894' W 5° 57. 381'

Mural	Location	GPS
Black Taxis	Ardoyne Ave/Havana Walk	N 54° 36. 894' W 5° 57. 357'
Martin Meehan	Havana Walk	N 54° 37. 072' W 5° 57. 765'
Rhythm of Time	Ardoyne Ave/Havana Gds	N 54° 36. 892' W 5° 57. 309'
Resistance	Ardoyne Ave/Havana Gds	N 54° 36. 891' W 5° 57. 294'
Ardoyne Bone Boxing Club	Ardoyne Ave/Jamaica Rd	N 54° 36. 891' W 5° 57. 292'
Hunger Strikers	Louisa Ct/Ardilea Cl	N 54° 36. 909' W 5° 57. 060'
Sandy Row: Past and Present	Sandy Row/Stroud St	N 54° 35. 362' W 5° 56. 086'
Titanic Workers	Donegall Rd/Combermere St	N 54° 35. 371' W 5° 54. 154'
Alex 'Hurricane' Higgins	Donegall Rd	N 54° 35. 333' W 5° 56. 177'
Alex 'Hurricane' Higgins	Donegall Rd/Abingdon Dr	N 54° 35. 341' W 5° 56. 565'
George Best	Sandy Row/Blythe St	N 54° 35. 390' W 5° 56. 220's
Robert Duggan	Sandy Row/Blythe St	N 54° 35. 390' W 5° 56. 220'
Linfield FC: Weavers to Winners	Blyth St/Felt St	N 54° 35. 433' W 5° 53. 500'
Common Sense	Roden St/Lemberg St	N 54° 35. 433' W 5° 53. 961'
UVF	Tavanagh St/Frenchpark St	N 54° 35. 183' W 5° 57. 381'
Queen Elizabeth	Rockview St/Frenchpark St	N 54° 35. 181' W 5° 57. 351'
Young Citizen Volunteers	Kitchner Dr/Kitchner St	N 54° 35. 254' W 5° 57. 093'
UDA	Donegall Rd/Kilburn St	N 54° 35. 321' W 5° 57. 249'
Battle of the Somme	Donegall Rd/Kilburn St	N 54° 35. 321' W 5° 57. 249'
Women Too	Kilburn St/Broadway	N 54° 35. 238' W 5° 57. 274'
King Billy	Tavanagh St/Broadway	N 54° 35. 259' W 5° 57. 399'

Mural	Location	GPS	
Ulster Covanant	Tavanagh St/Broadway	N 54° 35. 254'	W 5° 57. 343'
Teenage Dreams	Bridge End	N 54° 36. 054'	W 5° 54. 657'
Ship of Dreams	Newtownards Road/Wolff Cl	N 54° 36. 018'	W 5° 54. 451'
No More	Newtownards Rd/Wolff Cl	N 54° 36. 018'	W 5° 54. 451'
You Are Never Too Old	Newtownards Road	N54° 35. 998'	W5° 54. 408'
For Valour	Newtownards Road	N 54° 36. 004'	W 5° 54. 308'
HMS Belfast	Newtownards Rd/Tower St	N 54° 35. 973'	W 5° 54. 237'
Dream, Seek, Educate, Achieve	Newtownards Rd/Susan St	N 54° 35. 982'	W 5° 54. 300'
Conflict and Nationality	Newtownards Road	N 54° 35. 971'	W 5° 54. 217'
War and Peace	Newtownards Rd/Lendrick St	N 54° 35. 947'	W 5° 54. 033'
East Belfast Protestant Boys	Newtownards Rd/Hemp St	N 54° 35. 896'	W 5° 53. 637'
36th Ulster Division	Newtownards Rd/St Leonards Cres	N 54° 35. 941'	W 5° 53. 983'
Never Forget the Past	Newtownards Rd/Derwent St	N 54° 35. 944'	W 5° 53. 935'
East Belfast Remembers	Newtownards Road	N 54° 35. 944'	W 5° 53. 935'
East Belfast UVF	Newtownards Road	N 54° 35. 931'	W 5° 53. 827'
The Right to Defend Yourself	Newtownards Road	N 54° 35. 917'	W 5° 53. 848'
Titanic	Newtownards Rd/Dee St	N 54° 35. 922'	W 5° 53. 835'
Narnia	Dee St/Pansy St	N 54° 36. 025'	W 5° 53. 802'
Shipyard Workers	Harkness Pde	N 54° 36. 156'	W 5° 53. 728'
Ulster Division	Newtownards Rd/Hunt St	N 54° 35. 901'	W 5° 53. 676'
East Belfast Protestant Boys	Newtownards Road	N 54° 35. 896'	W 5° 53. 645'
UVF	Inverwood Ct	N 54° 35. 922'	W 5° 53. 835'

93

Mural	Location	GPS
The Great War	Inverary Dr/Station Rd	N 54° 35. 922' W 5° 53. 835'
Years of Sacrifice	Carlingford St/Ardenvohr St	N 54° 35. 326' W 5° 54. 223'
Ulster Division	Carlingford St	N 54° 35. 322' W 5° 54. 223'
Carson's Volunteers	Carlingford St	N 54° 35. 322' W 5° 54. 223'
Cosy Somme Association	Woodstock Rd/Ogilvie St	N 54° 35. 244' W 5° 53. 024'
Templemore Avenue Primary School	Major St/Parker St	N 54° 35. 877' W 5° 54. 087'
Loyalist Prisoners	Templemore Ave/Harvey Ct	N 54° 35. 839' W 5° 54. 105'
Gertrude Star Flute Band 1960-2011	Templemore Ave/Martin St	N 54° 35. 822' W 5° 54. 094'
Gertrude Star Flute Band	Templemore Ave/Martin St	N 54° 35. 822' W 5° 54. 094'
East Belfast Historical & Cultural Society	Templemore Ave/Thorndyke St	N 54° 35. 715' W 5° 54. 037'
Tim Collins	Beersbridge Rd/Kenbaan St	N 54° 35. 565' W 5° 53. 973'
UDA	Lord St/Chatsworth St	N 54° 35. 708' W 5° 53. 966'
Belfast Giants	Lord Street/Constance St	N 54° 35. 719' W 5° 53. 974'
Boxing Through the Generations	Templemore St	N 54° 35. 758' W 5° 53. 868'
Drugs Destroy Lives	Granton Pk	N 54° 35. 344' W 5° 49. 824'
UFF Tullycarnet	Kings Rd	N 54° 35. 317' W 5° 49. 828'
James Magennis	Kings Rd	N 54° 35. 293' W 5° 49. 764'
Ulster Division 1914-18 VCs	Cappagh Gds	N 54° 34. 453' W 5° 54. 003'
George Best	Cappagh Gds	N 54° 34. 455' W 5° 53. 977'
Micky Devine	Chemical St	N 54° 35. 920' W 5° 54. 586'
Sean Martin	Beechfield St/Mountpottinger Rd	N 54° 35. 877' W 5° 54. 528'

Mural	Location	GPS
Charlie Monaghan: Easter 1916	Mountpottinger Rd	N 54° 35. 896' W 5° 54. 582'
Short Strand IRA Volunteers	Mountpottinger Rd	N 54° 35. 896' W 5° 54. 582'
East Belfast	Beechfield St/Edgar St	N 54° 35. 851' W 5° 54. 341'
IRA Active Service Unit	Friendly Way	N 54° 35. 695' W 5° 55. 221'
Celtic F.C.	Stewart St/Friendly St	N 54° 35. 646' W 5° 55. 084'
James Largey	Friendly Row	N 54° 35. 665' W 5° 55. 378'
Albion Star	Stanfield Pl	N 54° 35. 646' W 5° 55. 288'
Drumcree	Ormeau Rd/Artana St	N 54° 35. 037' W 5° 55. 326'
Union Flag/UVF	Donegall Pass/Charlotte St	N 54° 35. 415' W 5° 55. 622'
YCV/UVF Donegall Pass	Donegall Pass/Walnut St	N 54° 35. 400' W 5° 55. 618'
William of Orange	Donegall Pass/Oak St	N 54° 35. 389' W 5° 55. 728'
Seige of Derry	Donegall Pass/Oak St	N 54° 35. 389' W 5° 55. 728'
36th Ulster Division	Donegall Pass/Apsley St	N 54° 35. 409' W 5° 55. 735'
Thiepval Tower	Donegall Pass/Pine St	N 54° 35. 390' W 5° 55. 650'
UVF	Donegall Pass/Pine St	N 54° 35. 390' W 5° 55. 650'
Young Conquerers Flute Band	Donegall Pass/Pine St	N 54° 35. 390' W 5° 55. 650'
UVF	Derry Hill/Derrycoole Way Rathcoole	N 54° 40. 058' W 5° 55. 656'
Red Hand Commandos	Derrycoole Way, Rathcoole	N 54° 40. 138' W 5° 55. 356'
Queen Elizabeth	Owenreagh Way/Eastway Rarhcoole	N 54° 40. 092' W 5° 55. 008'
First World War	Mount Vernon Pk/Mount Vernon Gds	N 54° 37. 953' W 5° 55. 662'
Prepared for Peace, Ready for War	Mount Vernon Rd	N 54° 37. 870' W 5° 55. 437'

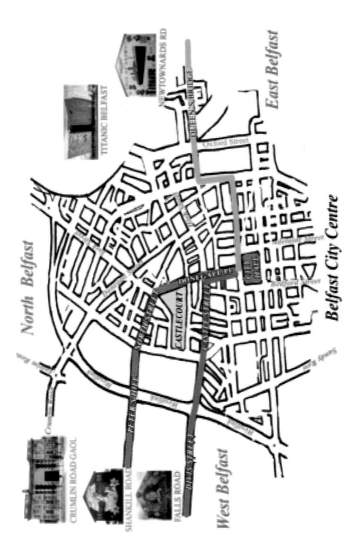